D1577977

Soccer Coaching:

A Step-by-Step Guide on How to Lead Your Players, Manage Parents, and Select the Best Formation

Dylan Joseph

Soccer Coaching: A Step-by-Step Guide on How to Lead Your Players, Manage Parents, and Select the Best Formation

By: Dylan Joseph
© 2019

All Rights Reserved

WAIT!

Wouldn't it be nice to have the one-hour practice discussed in this book, plus a questionnaire for your players' parents, on an easy two-page printout to take to the field? Well, here's your chance!

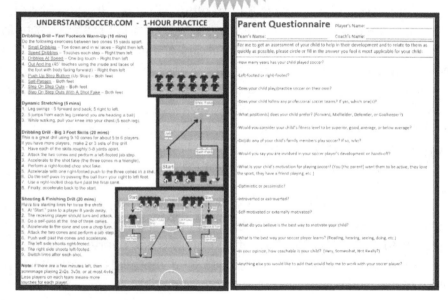

Go to This Link for an **Instant** Two-Page Printout:
UnderstandSoccer.com/free-printout

These FREE guides are simply a thank you for purchasing this book. This two-page printout will ensure that you are ready for practice and will help gauge how interested in soccer your players and their parents are.

Soccer Coaching:
A Step-by-Step Guide on How to Lead Your Players, Manage Parents,
and Select the Best Formation
All Rights Reserved
October 7, 2019
Copyright © 2019 Understand, LLC
Dylan@UnderstandSoccer.com
Printed in the United States of America

No part of this book may be reproduced or transmitted in any form or by any means, electronic or mechanical, including but not limited to photocopying, recording, or by any information storage and retrieval system, without the written permission of Understand, LLC.

The information provided within this book is for general informational and educational purposes only and does not constitute an endorsement of any websites or other sources. If you apply the ideas contained in this book, then you are taking full responsibility for your actions. There are no representations or warranties, expressed or implied, about the completeness, accuracy, reliability, suitability, or availability of the information, products, or services contained in this book for any purpose. The author does not assume and hereby disclaims all liability to any party for any loss, damage, or disruption caused by errors or omissions, whether the errors or omissions are a result of accident, negligence, or any other cause.

Any use of this information is at your own risk. The methods described in this book are the author's personal thoughts. They are not intended to be a definitive set of instructions for every single player. You may discover that other methods and materials accomplish the same result. This book contains information that is intended to help readers become better-informed consumers of soccer knowledge. Always consult your physician for your individual needs before beginning any new exercise program. This book is not intended to be a substitute for the medical advice of a licensed physician.

Table of Contents

Dedication

This book is dedicated to all the coaches who are reading this information to increase their confidence, to learn how to work effectively with different players, and to improve communication with their players' parents. Coaching can be tough, given all the different things you must balance at once. I applaud you for the countless hours you have put in, and the minimal recognition you have received in the tiring but rewarding position you hold on your soccer team.

Also, this book is dedicated to my past soccer coaches: Aaron Byrd, Derin White, Alan Placek, Franco Mancini, George Stewart, Josh VanHouten, and Tom VanHouten. These coaches provided considerable guidance over the years and made me into the player and trainer I am today. Thanks a ton!

Preface

Average coaches only focus on game-specific tactics. Great coaches know that working well with parents, gaining players' trust, and developing strong game-specific tactics are a must. Great coaches know there are a million things to focus on but determining which 20% of those things will produce at least 80% of the results is key to being the most efficient coach possible.

This book is not meant to be a complete guide on coaching. This book's main goal is to reveal the many key areas that can make a huge difference and are relatively easy to implement. This book will give you the tips, tricks, tweaks, and techniques to become a coach whom parents want to work with, soccer players love to play for, and all the other coaches in the league envy.

Understand that changing one or two things may help improve your team's game, but once you start implementing most (if not all) of the techniques described in this book, you will see a significant improvement in your team's performance on the field. Remember, the knowledge in this book is only helpful when applied.

INDIVIDUAL SOCCER PLAYER'S PYRAMID

If you want to improve your players' skills, your team's confidence, or your squads' abilities, then it is essential to understand where this book fits into the bigger picture of developing a soccer player. In the image above, you can see that the most critical field-specific things to work on are at the base of the Individual Soccer Player's Pyramid. The pyramid is a quality outline to improve an individual soccer player's game. All the elements in the pyramid, and the items surrounding it, will play a meaningful part in becoming a better player, but certain skills should be taught and mastered first before moving on to the others.

You will notice that passing and receiving is at the foundation of the pyramid. This is because if your players can receive and make a pass in soccer, then they will be useful. Even though they may not consistently score, dispossess the other team, or dribble through several opponents, they will still have the fundamental tools needed to play the sport and contribute to the team.

As you move one layer up, you will find yourself deciding how to progress as a coach. The pyramid is created with players in mind because every soccer player and position has different needs. Therefore, when choosing which path to teach first, you should **consider which skillset you want your players to learn first**.

For example, if you want your players to work on scoring, then consider starting your route on the second layer of the pyramid with shooting and finishing. Otherwise, you can start by teaching your players dribbling and foot skills because learning the proper technique is crucial to dribbling the ball well. It is often necessary for a soccer player to use a foot skill to protect the ball from the other team or advance the ball up the field to place their team in a favorable position to score.

You may instead want to proceed from passing and receiving to defending. Keeping the other team off the scoreboard is not an easy task. Developing a defender's mindset, teaching which way to push a forward, showing your players how to position their body, and ensuring that they use the correct form for headers is critical for a defender on the back line who wants to prevent goals.

Be sure to finish teaching all three areas in the second layer of the pyramid before progressing up the pyramid. Dribbling and defending the ball (not just shooting) are useful for an attacker; shooting and defending (not just dribbling) are helpful for a midfielder, while shooting and dribbling (not just defending) are helpful for a defender. Having well-rounded knowledge of the skills needed for each position is important for all soccer players. Shooting and finishing, dribbling and foot skills, and defending are often more beneficial for soccer players to learn first, so focus on these before spending time on the upper areas of the pyramid.

Once you have improved your players' skills in the first and second tiers of the pyramid, then you can move up to fitness. It is difficult to go through a passing/dribbling/finishing drill for a few minutes without noticing that your players are out of breath. However, as they practice everything below the fitness category in the pyramid, their fitness and strength will naturally increase. Performing technical drills will allow soccer players to increase their fitness naturally. This will reduce the need to focus exclusively on running for fitness.

Coming from the perspective of both a soccer player and trainer, I know that constantly focusing on running is not as fulfilling and does not create long-lasting improvements, whereas emphasizing shooting capabilities, foot skills, and defending knowledge will create long-lasting change. Often, coaches who focus on running their players in practice are also coaches who want to improve their team but have limited knowledge of many of the soccer-specific topics that would quickly increase their players' abilities. Soccer fitness does not only include endurance; it also addresses how to run with agility and speed, and how to develop strength and power with weight training, while using stretching to improve flexibility. All these tools put together will lead to a well-rounded soccer player.

Finally, we travel to the top of the pyramid, which involves tryouts. Although tryouts occur only 1-2 times per year, they have a huge impact on whether a player makes the team or is left out of the lineup. Tryouts can cause intense anxiety if players do not know how to make sure that they stand out from their competitors and are confident from the start.

If you have not read the *Understand Soccer* series book, *Soccer Training*, then it is highly recommended that you do so to gain the general knowledge of crucial topics within the areas of the pyramid. Picking up a copy of this book will act as a good gauge to see how much you know about each topic, which will further help determine if a book later in the series will be beneficial to you.

The last portion of the pyramid is made up of the areas that surround it. Although these skills and topics cannot be addressed by a player's physical abilities, they still play key roles in rounding out a complete soccer player. For example, having a supportive parent/guardian or two is beneficial, as they can provide transportation to and from games, the necessary equipment, the team fees, expenses for individual training, and most importantly, encouragement. Having a quality coach whose teachings and drills help the individual learn how their performance and skills fit into the team's big picture will help a lot, too.

Getting enough sleep is critical to have enough energy during practices and on game days, in addition to recovering from training and games. Also, appropriate soccer nutrition will increase your players' energy and endurance, help them achieve the ideal physique, and significantly aid in their recovery.

Understanding soccer positions will help you determine if a specific role is well-suited for one of your player's skills. It is important to know that there are additional types of specific positions—not just forwards, midfielders, and defenders.

Finally, your players must develop an unshakable mindset. This mindset will help them prepare for game situations, learn how to deal with other players, and become mentally tough enough to not worry about circumstances they cannot control, such as the type of field they play on, the officiating, or the weather.

In conclusion, the pyramid is a great visual aid to consider when choosing which areas to focus on next as a coach. However, remember that a team's pyramid may look slightly different, based on which tactics the players can handle, and which approach you decide to use for games.

Now that you know where this book plays into the bigger picture, let us begin. Remember that if there are any words or terms whose meaning you are unsure of; reference the glossary at the back of the book.

Finally, if you enjoy this book, then please leave a review on Amazon to let me know.

Introduction

The overarching objective of this book is to improve the soccer IQ of coaches and trainers. This book details various coaching styles, as well as ways to earn the team's respect and motivate them to work hard. This book does not cover the technical aspects of soccer, such as how to pass the ball, shoot properly, or perform a foot skill. Other books in the *Understand Soccer* series cover these subjects and are also available on Amazon.com.

Although the book cover is black and white, the concepts within are not quite so black and white. Each individual player is different, and although one concept can be used for many players, **most guidelines are not effective for all players**. If you are constantly searching for the one thing that will change everything, then understand there often is no "silver bullet" that will allow everything else to fall perfectly into place. As the coach, you are the leader of the team and should therefore lead by example. The harder you work, the harder your team will work. There is no perfect way to coach, and it normally takes time to find the style that works best for you and motivates your players.

Finally, this book reveals the "Big 3" formations used by many coaches and explains other common variations to help you determine whether your current formation is best for your team or if another formation would produce better results. Choosing your formation can be the deciding factor that achieves success.

Additionally, this book has many bonus takeaways, including great ways to deal with parents, and how to overcome the occasional difficult player.

The format of the book is assembled into three sections:
1. Topics Unrelated to Practice
2. Topics Related to Practice
3. Formations

Section 1

Topics Unrelated to Practice

Chapter 1

Determine Your Coaching Style

One of the most productive things you can do before the season even starts is determine what type of coach you want to be. Do you want to be fair and give everyone equal amounts of playing time? Is your main goal to win? Is your main goal to build your players' character, confidence, and soccer skills? Do you have a preferred formation/playstyle, or will you pick one based on your players' abilities?

Coaching styles are often broken down into three major categories:

1. How you handle your relationship with your players and their parents.
2. How you select your playstyle and team formations.
3. How you advance your players' technical skills.

The first section will focus on how to handle your relationship with your players and their parents. In the two sections that follow, how to approach practice and implement different playstyles and formations will be discussed. To advance your players' technical skills, I recommend using the *Understand Soccer* series books on shooting and finishing, dribbling and foot skills, passing and receiving, and defending.

Before we get into the advantages and disadvantages of different approaches that you can take with your players and their parents, first make sure that you have thought about the main goal for your team, and then communicate your expectations to your players and their parents at tryouts (if applicable) or at the beginning of the season. Depending on the type of team you coach, and the age group of your players, telling the parents your style of coaching may make it easier for them to understand what you expect of their children and whether your team is a good fit for their child.

Remember that certain players and/or parents may not relate to the main objective that you are trying to achieve, and they may seek other teams to play for instead. If this happens, it may feel like they are rejecting you and your style. In reality, you are merely setting expectations for everyone at the outset of the season so that when the going gets tough, everyone will have agreed on the main objective beforehand. It is much better if the players and parents are onboard with the aspirations you have set than if they seek to undermine you halfway through the season because they expected one thing, but you delivered another. **Therefore, setting your overarching coaching goal(s) at the beginning of the season will make most of your decisions easier because there will usually be an obvious way to correctly handle the situation, based on your goal(s).**

For example, let us consider that your coaching style prioritizes winning, and a parent of one of your players is complaining that their child does not receive enough playing time. In this situation, you can point back to the beginning of the season, when you clearly set your expectations for the team which meant that playing time would be based on wins, and there would not be equal playing time for each player. If the parent does not like your decision, then you can reply, "Although it can be frustrating and at times it may not seem like it is working out perfectly for all parties, we did agree on the goals, values, and expectations at the beginning of the season. I am simply continuing to coach in this fashion, as it would be unfair to the other parents, players, and myself to change our objectives and expectations halfway through the season." **Fortunately, setting these expectations at the beginning of the season will reduce the number of conversations like this.**

Instead, maybe your goal is to build your players' character. In this situation, if a penalty is awarded in favor of your team, but your player informs you that they were not fouled, then you can easily tell the referee that there should not have been a penalty kick awarded and to let the other team take a goal kick instead.

In conclusion, setting expectations early for players and parents will make your decisions much more black-and-white and will reduce the number of frustrating conversations you will have with yourself, your team, and their parents. Set expectations at the beginning of the season, so the players and parents will know where you stand. If opting out of your team is an option in your league, then clearly expressed and understood expectations will allow them to do so if their goals do not align with your objectives.

To help you further understand the parents' expectations and their level of involvement with their child's soccer pursuits, as well as how to discover your players' personalities at the beginning of the season, grab your two-page free printout at UnderstandSoccer.com/free-printout, which includes a ready-made parent questionnaire to hand out during your first team meeting.

YouTube: If you would like to see a video on how to pick your coaching style, then consider watching the *Understand Soccer* YouTube video: *How to Pick Your Soccer Coaching Philosophy*.

Chapter 2

Get Hyped!

As mentioned in the previous chapter, it is important to determine the type of relationship you intend to have with your players at the beginning of the season, so your expectations can be set early on. **One highly recommended suggestion— especially for younger players—is to be "hyped."** Being hyped means you are your players' biggest advocate, you reward good behavior, you are quick to show praise, and you offer only constructive criticism.

Something most coaches do not use enough is the high five. In a time when hugging a player or giving them a pat on the back can be considered inappropriate, a high five is the happy medium between a hug and no contact whatsoever. After a high five (i.e., physical contact), the brain releases four feel-good chemicals: endorphins, oxytocin, serotonin, and dopamine. In contrast, when a player is faced with criticism and disdain, the stress chemical called cortisol is released instead.

During the contact of a high five, dopamine in the player triggers the release of even more oxytocin than just praise alone. This creates a bond between the coach and the player, while also reinforcing good behavior and making the player much more receptive to feedback. Obviously, you need to be a coach first, but it often will not hurt to be a friend, too. Players play harder for coaches they like and respect.

Consider Jürgen Klopp, who has coached Borussia Dortmund and Liverpool. Whenever his team scores huge goals, he has been known to run onto the field to the goal-scorer to celebrate with the team. Keep in mind that he has been fined for this, so I do not recommend doing it, but it does provide a great example of how fully invested Klopp is in his team. His charismatic nature allows him to be the premier coach in any league because he realizes that positive physical contact and becoming hyped shows his players that they are unified in achieving their dreams. Showing how much he cares has earned his players' respect and resulted in him taking the club team Liverpool to back-to-back Champions League Finals, including a victory in the 2019 Finals.

In her book, *Mindset,* Carol S. Dweck, Ph.D. presents numerous studies in which thousands of children showed how to improve players' abilities over the course of a season. Dweck insists on **praising your players for their hard work—*not* their intelligence**. When a coach praises their players for their intelligence, the player will look to complete more easy tasks to show off that intelligence. Because you communicated that their intelligence is most important, they will shy away from harder tasks that move them outside their comfort zone. Instead, praise your players for their effort and hard work, and they will seek challenges that demonstrate their willingness to work hard and develop.

Finally, remember that using constant criticism will only make your players mentally criticize you. Using constant praise will ensure that no mental burdens will slow the development of your players' soccer abilities. However, it is not suggested that you provide no criticism at all. You are the coach, after all, and your job is to direct your players towards improvement. Therefore, if they are doing something wrong, then praising their mistake will not help them grow. Instead, positively redirect them and make sure that you give thoughtful feedback, so your players will trust you, agree with you, and immediately implement your advice into their game. A chapter later in this book reveals exactly how to do this.

Chapter 3

Top 10 Non-Technical Topics That Every Coach Should Teach

1. **Make sure your team** practices using their opposite foot, not so much that they are as good with it as their dominant foot, but so they can still be a threat if the defender gives them space to their opposite foot. A player who cannot shoot with their opposite foot is one of the easiest players to stop because a defender can cut off their path up the field to their dominant foot without worrying about the player shooting with their opposite foot. Plus, a player who can shoot and pass with both feet will receive a huge confidence boost!

2. **Work on your team's weaknesses until they are adequate, but make sure you emphasize and practice your team's strengths, too**. For example, consider the next image. This team is outstanding at shooting, good at defending and passing, okay at dribbling, and needs significant improvement on headers. In this case, the coach should consider their team's strengths and weaknesses. The coach should focus on improving their dribbling and headers to the minimum line. From there, the coach should emphasize their shooting abilities to maximize their strengths. Too many coaches try to focus on everything at once, so their team can become well-balanced.

However, using this approach ensures that the team will become "jacks of all trades and masters of none." Instead, emphasize your team's strengths by making game plans that highlight them and minimize their weaknesses by practicing their weaknesses just enough to ensure that your team is hugely successful.

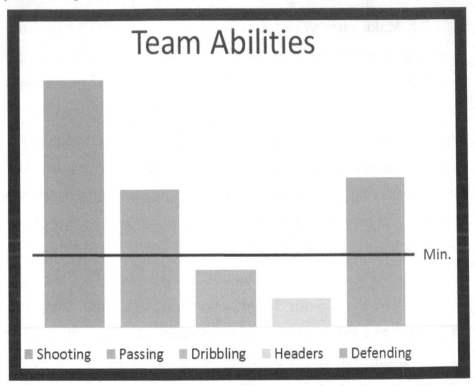

3. **Make sure your players know to tell their teammates** where they want the ball to be passed using **hand motions that are not visible to the defender.** They should not expect the pass that they want if they cannot tell the person who is passing the ball exactly where they want it. **Recommend that they point with their hands.** I suggest opening their hand in front of them if they want the ball at their

feet, to the right if they want it slightly in front of them and to their right, or to the left if they want it slightly in front of them and to the left. Similarly, if they want the ball played well in front of them, they should point to the spot on the field, so they can sprint to the ball and receive it in stride.

4. **Insist that your players** demand the ball, **not ask for the ball. They should yell for the ball, not call for the ball.** These shifts in wording (i.e., "demand" vs. "ask" and "yell" vs. "call") do a few excellent things for your players who want to receive a pass or be played a through ball. Demanding the ball and yelling for it with conviction will ensure that your players know their teammates want the ball and will do something productive when they receive it.

5. When a player's back is facing the direction in which they need to travel, they should look behind themselves just before receiving a pass from a teammate. This will allow them to turn with the ball quickly and confidently, which will help them score more goals and create more assists for your team. It cannot be stressed enough that your players should look over their shoulders when preparing to receive a pass. Depending on the situation, it may be best for them to just hold the ball and wait for support. A quick look will let them know where they should push the ball—or even if they should request a pass at all. **Encourage them to avoid twisting at the hips to look behind**

themselves because this takes too much time. Instead, teach them to turn their head at the neck to take a swift look at the field, and the players behind them. If they have space to attack, then they should yell for the ball and demand that it be passed to them.

6. **Remind your players not to worry about making mistakes**—especially during practices and scrimmages. Those are the times to make the mistakes, so your players can learn and develop their skills well enough to be used in a game. Remember that most people must learn from their own mistakes, so let them make mistakes in low-risk environments. Have your players encourage each other. Nothing discourages creativity and team chemistry more than teammates who criticize each other.

7. **Spend as much practice time as possible with a ball at your players' feet.** This will make them more confident with the ball. The best coaches who develop players are those who make each player in the system better—especially for 12-year-olds and younger. The more time you spend on tactics, the less time you can spend on the development of each player's skills. Focusing on team tactics is acceptable for high school, college, and pro-level teams. However, through the developmental ages, you should focus on each individual player, and their abilities with the ball. This will make them better players in any coach's

system. Emphasize drills with lots of repetitions and lots of touches with the ball.

8. **Avoid placing blame on any individuals on your team.** It takes the whole team to win and the whole team to lose. Players will multiply the energy that you give them. If you yell at them, then they will build resentment and be afraid to make more mistakes, so their growth will come to a screeching halt. Usually, the player who made the mistake already knows the effect it will have on the team, so by drawing more attention to it, you are only shutting them down mentally in the near-term and giving their teammates an excuse for not working to overcome the error.

9. **Raise your expectations.** Players and students often perform to the expectations placed on them. A Harvard professor named Robert Rosenthal performed a study in which he told teachers that certain students in their classes had been tested and were determined to be highly intelligent. However, these students were all selected at random, and no student did anything to distinguish themselves from the others. For the next several months, the teachers treated these students differently. The students who were treated as smarter advanced quicker than the other kids in the class because their teachers had higher expectations of them.

10. **Give your players homework.** It can help double your players' touches. It is easiest to emphasize their touches with homework because it can be done with a soccer ball in any amount of space and teammates are not necessary. Working on toe taps, foundations, shot fakes, fast footwork, and foot skills are easy to do. As your players age, they may have access to gyms, workout programs, and at-home DVDs to work on strength, flexibility, and speed, as well.

The Villarreal, Arsenal, and Paris Saint-Germain coach, Unai Emery, is best known for being a student of the game. He takes preparation very seriously by learning the best tactics for his players and assigning considerable amounts of homework. He gives his players USB drives with assignments on them. There was one particular player whom he feared was not taking the homework seriously, so he gave that player a blank USB drive. When Emery asked the player how his homework went, the player said it went well and was completed. Because there was nothing on the USB drive, the player was reprimanded for not doing the homework. Similar to how assigning homework helped Emery determine which players were dedicated, it too can help you determine levels of commitment and double your players' number of touches each week.

Bonus Tip: Arthur Skaer spent over five decades as a soccer player, and over two decades as a coach. He was voted

Coach of the Year for Virginia's largest soccer organization. During each game he coaches, he makes one or two of his bench players record statistics of what is occurring on the field. Specifically, they record shots taken, completed passes, goal kicks, corner kicks, throw-ins, and goalkeeper saves.

stats book?

Having one or two players (record statistics) while they are not on the field provides two major benefits: (1) The bench players will be much more engaged and will pay attention, which will further their learning of the game; and (2) You will get meaningful data from games to determine your team's progress and potentially uncover areas that need significant improvement. In addition to the statistics mentioned above, feel free to include additional metrics that you would like to track for your team.

If you are interested in learning more technical tips, consider picking up these four books in the *Understand Soccer* series: *Soccer Shooting & Finishing, Soccer Dribbling & Foot Skills, Soccer Passing & Receiving,* and *Soccer Defending.*

YouTube: If you would like to see a video on the top 10 non-technical ideas to teach, then consider watching the *Understand Soccer* YouTube video: *Soccer Coaching Points.*

Chapter 4

Clock Management

Soccer is a sport with a fixed amount of time. Unlike basketball and hockey, there are no timeouts in soccer. It is both a competition against the other team, and a race against the clock. Due to its set amount of time, managing the clock is essential. Often, games will have a scoreboard, so all players, coaches, and spectators will know roughly how much time is left. But it is at the referee's discretion to add time for game stoppages for injuries, discipline, and other unplanned stoppages of play. **If there is no scoreboard with the time, then a coach or two on your team should use their own watch to ensure that they correctly manage the remaining time.** Let us discuss a few ways to control the clock and prevent goals by the other team.

You should consider your team's playstyle, and the tactic you have chosen, but one of the worst things a team can do is go purely into a defensive mode after scoring an early goal. The goal will have just generated momentum for your team and switching to a defensive mindset will limit your team's ability to provide a cushion of two or three goals. However, if your team has a great forward, and a solid defense, then you should absolutely look for opportunities to counterattack. Just avoid limiting your team's playstyle too early in the game.

The more you focus on defense early in a game, the more relaxed you will become. This will increase the chance of the opposing team closing the passing lanes down as your team's defense passes the ball and the other team may eventually intercept a pass in a position that can create a quick counterattack. **In short, playing very defensively too early in a game is a risk you should avoid.**

I have a good friend and teammate named Toni Sinistaj, who is always very ungenerous with restarts when his team is ahead. He does whatever he can to buy his team more time by taking longer to give the ball to the other team or making sure that his team is in position before giving the ball to the person who will take the throw-in. **He does a great job of avoiding placing his team in a disadvantaged position if he has the power to do something about it.**

I always give him a hard time for using this tactic anytime I am on the other team in a practice, scrimmage, or pickup game because I am trying to help my team win. However, I respect him and his strategy because it helps his team and is entirely within the rules. **However, remember that if you intend to use this strategy, your player must avoid taking too long because they may receive a yellow card from the referee for delaying the game.** This seemingly petty tactic might not be received well by the other team but remember that you are playing a competitive sport and using clock management strategies can be the difference between winning and losing a game.

By promptly giving the other team the ball during a game, you are letting them win a small battle. Do not retrieve the ball for the opposition because that will save them time and energy. Sure, allowing them to win these small battles will not often be detrimental to your team or lead to goals for the other team. However, a few times a season, these situations will turn into goals for the other team if they are paying better attention and are ready to act rapidly. **This is also an excellent opportunity for you to help your team catch their breath for a few seconds if they have been running nonstop.** Simply holding the ball for a bit longer or dropping it to the ground can buy your team some added physical and mental rest because the opposition must spend time collecting the ball.

If you are looking to kill time during a game, passing among the defenders and midfielders on your team is terrific. Granted, your team must have the talent to maintain possession. **If they do not, then in the last few minutes of the game, consider kicking the ball up the field or having one of your best players dribble the ball to the corner flag to prevent the other team from gaining possession.** Tactics like this may be considered a bit unsportsmanlike but are certainly within the rules of the game and should be considered when your team is looking for any advantage to run out the clock and win.

In summary, use appropriate clock management techniques when looking to sustain a lead in a game. Avoid quickly giving the ball to the other team when it goes out of bounds. Make them use their energy to fetch the ball and give yourself enough time to be properly positioned. Pass the ball extensively to tire the other team's forwards and midfielders, as they are the players who will need the most energy towards the end of the game to score. Finally, when in uncomfortable situations, kick the ball past the other team's defensive line or run the ball to the corner flag to delay the other team from gaining possession.

Chapter 5

How to Deal with Difficult Players

Often, coaches will have at least one difficult soccer player on their team. They may be productive on the field, but their attitude will hold them back—both on the team and in life. **From time to time, the idea of removing this player from your team may cross your mind, but it should only be considered after you have tried numerous ways to resolve the situation.**

To start, your mindset about the situation will make a big difference. The energy you give to it will affect your

attitude and may lead you to fail at handling it. If you constantly think about how everything would be so much better if you did not have to deal with this player, then you may be looking at the situation with a narrow mind. Remember that you, as a coach, can use this situation to improve your communication abilities and conflict-resolution skills.

If you let yourself become emotionally drained by each situation that arises with the problem player, then you may become easily overwhelmed and miss the opportunity to learn. You can help a person with a difficult character trait, a person going through a difficult time, or a person who is stuck in frustrating circumstances. Remember that soccer is just one aspect of your players' lives, so not considering their whole situation will make it more difficult to resolve the problem.

Ideally, as a coach, you should not have to deal with this. However, choosing to be a person who helps a difficult player can give you a confidence boost that no winning season ever could. As best said by an ancient proverb, *"Ask not for a lighter burden but for broader shoulders."* **As a coach and fellow human being, do not stop trying.** Like most people, each individual on your team will respond in slightly different ways to criticism and positive reinforcement. They will deal with others and take responsibility differently.

Let us discuss several ways to improve the situation—or maybe even to completely resolve it. Consider the following when dealing with a difficult player:

1. Understand the real reason for their attitude.
2. Use positive reinforcement instead of criticism.
3. Increase their responsibility.
4. Do not forget about their parents.
5. Always keep your cool!

First, the most important thing to do when dealing with a difficult player is to understand why they are being difficult. Maybe their parents are going through a tough time. Maybe they have needs that are dissimilar to other kids their age. Maybe the player just really does not like you. Finding the root cause of their problematic behavior will significantly reduce the time it takes to understand how to best address the situation. Is there a certain scenario which provokes this behavior? Is the problem with another teammate? Is this a one-off situation that is totally out of character? Or has the player had similar difficult instances in the past? Use these questions and others to arrive at the root cause of their attitude.

Next, be a coach who is quick to reward the good. A coach who only points out mistakes and never congratulates their players when they perform well is difficult to play for over any significant period of time. This is why the legendary José Mourinho, coach of Porto, Chelsea, Inter Milan, Real Madrid, and Manchester United, tends to only last three years at each club. He uses criticism to shape his team during the first year to win a championship, then does okay in his second year, and is fired in his third year because his players become fed up with his criticism and do not want to hear it anymore. Only making negative comments about a player will only make them resent you and listen to very few of your suggestions.

If you have feedback that will significantly improve their game, then consider using a technique that is mentioned in the first book of the *Understand Soccer* series, *Soccer Training*. This is the "sandwich technique." First, compliment the player on something they are doing well. Keep the praise quick and straightforward, such as, "Good job approaching the ball diagonally when shooting." Then, give constructive feedback and explain why. For example, say, "If you plant your foot farther from the ball, it will allow you to turn your toe down and out more." Finally, end with another compliment, and an explanation, like, "Great job following through; it will ensure that you have plenty of power on your shot."

The sandwich method is crucial to help players who have a fixed mindset. By beginning with a compliment, you will break down any walls they have built up against constructive feedback.

By ending with a compliment, you will leave them feeling like they are doing most things correctly. **By providing constructive feedback in the middle of two compliments, you will make sure that they hear your message and have positive associations with it.** Include explanations for all three feedbacks to guarantee that the meaning of your message sticks with them, as well.

Also, consider giving the difficult player more responsibility on the team. Ask them to take a leadership role, so they will have skin in the game. If you hesitate to give them leadership responsibilities because they have not showed that they can handle themselves, remember that this new role will likely uncover abilities and skills that they have never used before, as well as give them a sense of purpose and ownership over the outcome of each practice and game.

For example, you may have a player who is often talkative while you are explaining drills. Pull this player aside and mention that they have great communication skills, and because they can easily connect with the other players, you have a special role for them—"group supervisor during drills." Tell them that this role involves kindly asking any other player who is talking to please be quiet until the drill demonstration is over. **This newly created role will give them a sense of purpose and help ensure that they keep quiet themselves during your demonstrations.**

Furthermore, you can speed up the process of dealing with a difficult player by increasing communication with their parent(s). Communicate expectations, inform them of the progress being made, the areas that still need improvement, and ensure that they are on your side. This will make resolving the difficult player's behavioral problems much easier. **Remember that if a parent disagrees with you, then they will undermine all your suggestions and important feedback if they tell their child the opposite of your suggestions once they are in the car or back at their home.**

Finally, you must stay calm on the outside—even if this player's actions frustrate you on the inside. Showing signs of anger or irritation will subconsciously reveal that you are not very emotionally mature, either. When the player sees your reaction, they will be even less likely to listen to advice from you. A coach who yells and becomes angry easily is also one who loses their players' respect quickly. Temperamental coaches will have a hard time controlling the locker room for the duration of the season.

In conclusion, your mindset as a coach will make dealing with a problematic player either much easier or significantly harder, depending on how you perceive the situation. Your coaching time is limited, so use it wisely to determine the root of the problematic player's behavioral issues. Use positive reinforcement to create change, while potentially increasing their role on the team. Understand that having their parents onboard with your plan will make handling the problem/opportunity a lot easier and will allow you to keep calm throughout the process. Finally, remember that you are the adult here, so make sure that you act like it. It is important to avoid the mindset trap of thinking, "It is my way or the highway."

Chapter 6

How to Deal with Difficult Parents

Every parent is different, so things may work for certain parents and not for others. However, the worst thing you can do is attempt one or two things, realize that they do not work, and then assume that the parent is crazy, that nothing will work for them, and/or that nothing you do will ever be good enough. Remember, developing your abilities as a coach is a process when it comes to both team and parent management.

As a coach, sometimes, you must deal with unruly parents. Many of us have had parents who thought their child was an absolute all-star. However, we as coaches know that they probably should not have even come off the bench, based on their subpar skills and performances. That said, those parents will be personally offended if you do not play their child as much as they think is appropriate. **When this happens, one of the worst things you can do is tell them that their kid is not good.**

One tactic that is constantly taught to salespeople is to agree with people—even when you may not really agree with their point of view. To the other person, their opinion is reasonable, and you will benefit tremendously by acknowledging it. You may be thinking that you are not a salesperson because you are a coach. However, you are always selling your abilities as a coach to parents. You are always proving your worth to the club directors. You are always selling your team tactics and techniques to your players. Therefore, although you are not a salesperson in the traditional sense of selling a product, you are still selling your leadership to the players and parents. You are still selling your belief in the greater good to all parties involved.

Therefore, beginning your conversation with a parent by immediately disagreeing with them is the equivalent of digging yourself into a hole. The trick is to be gentle and explain that, as a coach, you are trying to get the team to work together as efficiently as possible. Mention that their child's performance has been lackluster in practices, and that you reward effort in practices with playing time in games. **This statement does multiple things: (1) It lets the parent know that their kid will play if they improve and show more effort; (2) It gently lets them know that their child has room for improvement**, which will make it easier to see the need for additional training, courses, and books on how to help their child improve in soccer; and (3) **It helps you not appear to be the enemy** and conveys that you want the best result for the team.

If a parent dislikes you, and they have influence with the other parents, then you could develop a problem wherein many parents are against you, which may destroy the team's chemistry. Remind yourself that they are just parents letting you know they are distraught, and they feel that something is wrong and should be improved going forward. Be open to their feedback. Do not see them as the enemy. See their opinions as opportunities to grow. Improve your communication and learn from other people's perspectives because when you watch the game, you only have one set of eyes to view the action. While you are standing on the sideline, the parents may see additional things from the stands that you cannot fully view. If they bring their perspectives to you, then say, **"Thank you for the feedback,"** and let them know that you will surely consider what they said. This will ensure that they are on your side and looking out for your best interest, too. Keep the communication lines open, so they will continue to want their child on your team, and so that the team's dynamic will not be disrupted by parents who are distraught by their child's playtime, position, etc.

Above all, remember that this is still your team. You are the coach, and you may make some mistakes. Perhaps you played someone in an incorrect position, instead of one that would have been better for the team, but it was not apparent to you at the time. You are only human, and mistakes can happen. The best way to overcome mistakes is to learn and grow from them to limit their chances of happening again.

Section 2
Topics Related to Practice

Chapter 7

Deliberate Practice

Deliberate Practice > Purposeful Practice > Habitual Practice

If you have read the *Understand Soccer* series book, *Soccer Parenting*, this chapter will look similar to the chapter on deliberate practice in that book. However, because this book is for the coach, who is conducting the team's training sessions, this chapter will describe the coach's role in ensuring that their players practice deliberately. **As a coach, it is important that you do not practice just "to get touches."**

There are certain hot spots around the world that produce outstanding performers. Consider country singers from Tennessee, hockey players from Canada, and soccer players from Brazil (more on Brazilian soccer players later in this chapter). These hot beds for talent have training programs that involve deliberate practice.

Deliberate practice is systematic. Regular/habitual practice often means dribbling, shooting, and passing in ways that you have done before and are comfortable performing. **Deliberate practice requires attention and is conducted with the specific goal of improving performance by learning**

where the practice needs to go, and how to get there, step by step.

Habitual/regular practice (e.g., trying to juggle) is not as good as purposeful practice (e.g., setting a specific goal, such as juggling the ball 30 times in a row). **Purposeful practice is not as productive as deep/deliberate practice.** Deliberate practice is purposeful practice with the added information and knowledge to understand how to find your weak areas, and how to improve them to advance quickly by progressively focusing on the areas just outside your comfort zone (e.g., juggling 30 times in a row using the part of your feet nearest the tops of the toes to become better at settling the ball out of the air with an instinctual first touch).

When you first start playing soccer, everything is new, and just going through the reps will be a new experience in which considerable learning will occur. **But training in something you are good at doing with no meaningful plan to progress can result in overlooking small errors and missing opportunities to improve.**

Mindless activity is the enemy of deliberate practice. The danger of practicing the same thing again and again without focusing on making small improvements is believing you are becoming better because you are working on your soccer abilities. In reality, you are likely only reinforcing habits that still have room for improvement, thereby wasting valuable practice time. The natural tendency of the brain is to turn repeated actions into habits. **Deliberate practice breaks down the overall process into components, thereby allowing you to identify your weaknesses, work on different ways to improve them, and bring all the training together for significant improvement.**

As a soccer trainer, one of the biggest areas I see trainees struggle with—especially at a young age—is shooting a driven shot with the correct form. To succeed, a trainee must start diagonal to the ball, then plant a foot away from the ball. With the foot that the player is striking the ball with, they must have their toe down and out, with their knee facing the target, so they can use the bone of their foot. Afterwards, they must follow through, land on their shooting foot, bring their back leg forward, and point their hips in the direction they want to score. This is a lot for a child or adult to learn if this is the first time they are working through the steps.

Therefore, instead of working on all the steps at once, it is best to start the trainee planted about a foot away from the ball and focus on striking the ball with the bone of their foot. After 10-15 repetitions of becoming comfortable striking with the bone of their foot, I will then have them work on taking a step to correctly plant next to the ball and continue to strike with the bone of their foot. Then, after 10-15 repetitions of this step, I have them take a step to plant next to the ball, strike the ball with the bone of their foot, and then work on following through to land past the ball. **The process is like building blocks; they add in one additional step until they are comfortable enough to add another, until they are comfortable enough with all the steps to shoot driven shots with the correct form.**

From earlier in this chapter, you may be wondering how Brazil has so many well-developed soccer players. Well, the most popular form of soccer in Brazil is referred to as *"futebol de salão."* This is 5v5 soccer and is often played on a basketball court. During a game, each player has six times more touches than they would in an 11v11 soccer game. The professor of soccer at the University of São Paulo, Emilio Miranda, says it is Brazil's "laboratory of improvisation." **Taking many more touches with little room/time to make decisions will force players to improve their pattern recognition learn how to act in many soccer situations.**

When developing soccer skills, you should emphasize lots of repetitions and quick feedback. **To implement this methodology into your coaching style, make sure that multiple players have balls at their feet during drills, and instead of 11v11 scrimmages or 8v8 scrimmages, focus on**

3v3 or 2v2 scrimmages to ensure that more of your players are touching the ball at once.

In the next chapter, *"Example of a Great One-Hour Practice,"* the example practice starts with fast footwork, in which every player has a ball at their feet, followed by dribbling and shooting drills, in which each player continues to obtain many touches of the ball. To ensure quick feedback, after showing the example of each of the skills, stand at the jab step (i.e., body feint, as shown in the image) for the first lap and tell your players how they can improve their skill for the first set of four laps. During the next set of four laps, stand at the shot fake and instruct each soccer player in how they can perform that skill more efficiently. During the last set of four laps, stand at the self-pass and inform your players how they can perform that skill better. This drill will ensure that there are numerous repetitions and immediate feedback.

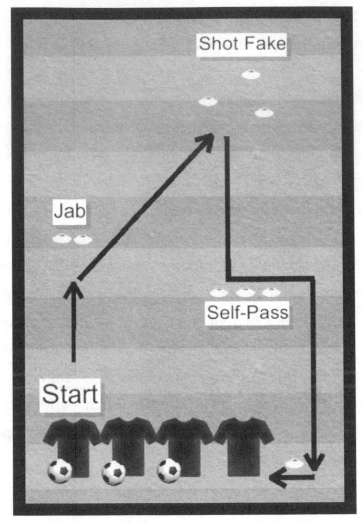

As a coach, it is important to understand the concept of deliberate practice to help your players advance their skills quickly and productively. If you are interested in learning more about deliberate practice, then consider picking up a copy of the book *Talent is Overrated* by **Geoff Colvin**. In the book, Colvin describes how Benjamin Franklin used deliberate practice to improve his writing skills, and Mozart used deliberate practice to become one of the greatest musicians of all time at a young age. He confirms the old saying that it takes about 10 years of deliberate practice to become an overnight sensation. Also, you may have heard others reference deliberate practice as the "10,000-Hour Rule," which states that it takes approximately 10,000 hours of deliberate practice to become great at anything.

YouTube: If you would like to see a video on coaching a deliberate practice, then consider watching the *Understand Soccer* YouTube video: *Deliberate Practice Soccer*.

Chapter 8

Example of a Great One-Hour Practice

Fast Footwork Warm-Up (10 mins)

Perform the following exercises between two cones set up 15 yards apart. Ideally, there should be two cones 15 yards apart for each player, so each player can experience as many touches as possible.

1. Small Dribbles – Toe Down and In – Right Foot, Then Left Foot

2. Speed Dribbles (i.e., Touches Every Step) – Toe Down and In Using Laces – Right Foot, Then Left Foot

3. Dribbles at Speed (i.e., One Big Touch) – Toe Down and In Using Laces – Right Foot, Then Left Foot

4. Out-and-Ins (i.e., 45° Touches Using the Inside and Laces of the Foot with Body Facing Forward) – Right Foot, Then Left Foot

5. Push-Up Stop-Bottom (i.e., Up-Stop) – Both Feet

6. Self-Passes – Both Feet

7. Step-On-Step-Outs – Both Feet

8. Step-On-Step-Outs with a Shot Fake – Both Feet

If some of these fast footwork items seem unclear, then consider subscribing to the *Understand Soccer* YouTube

Channel and watching the video: "*Soccer Dribbling Drills for Beginners*" to ensure that you understand how to perform each skill, as well as teach them. Additionally, a printable summary of this entire chapter is included in the free two-page printout at UnderstandSoccer.com/free-printout.

Dynamic Stretching (5 mins)

1. Leg Swings - 5 Forward and Back, 5 Right-to-Left (Perform with Both Legs)

2. 5 Jumps from Each Leg (Pretend You Are Heading a Ball)

3. While Walking, Pull Your Knee into Your Chest (5 Each Leg)

Dribbling Drill (20 mins)

The following drill is an excerpt from the *Understand Soccer* series book, *Soccer Dribbling & Foot Skills*. This is a great drill using 9-10 cones for about 5-6 players. If you have more players, then I recommend making multiple courses of this drill and dividing the group up amongst each course of cones.

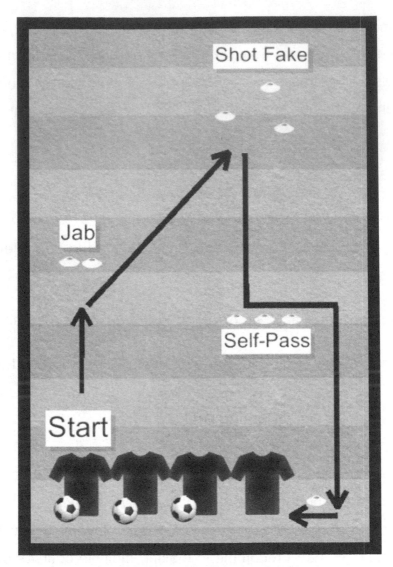

- Set up each of the skills roughly five yards apart.

- Attack the two cones and perform a left-footed jab step.

- Accelerate to the shot fake (i.e., the three cones in a triangle).

- Perform a right-footed chop shot fake.

- Accelerate with one push from your right foot to the three cones.

- Do a self-pass/la croqueta by passing the ball from your right foot to your left foot.
- Accelerate to the final cone and use a right-footed chop cut just past the cone.
- Finally, accelerate back to the start.

Note: Use only one push to accelerate to the next set of cones. Dribble with your head slightly up, not looking straight down at the ball. Make your shot fake look believable. This drill can be easily reversed to work on your skills in the opposite direction. Aim to have the players work to beat a specific time over three or four laps. Between sets, praise the players for what they did well and give constructive feedback on their mistakes.

Shooting and Finishing Drill (20 mins)

The following drill is great for an entire team. Forming two starting lines makes it so there are twice as many shots being taken. Twice as many shots means quicker improvement for the players who are going through the course, as well as great advancement for the goalkeeper, whose reaction time will be tested.

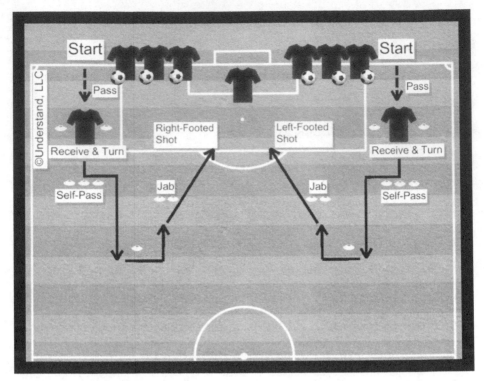

- Begin at the "Start" and pass to a player eight yards away.

- The receiving player should turn and attack the three cones.

- Do a self-pass/la croqueta from your right foot to your left foot (or vice versa.)

- Accelerate to the next singe cone and use a chop turn just past the cone.

- Attack the final two cones and perform a right/left-footed jab step.

- Take a big push past the cones and accelerate to the ball.

- Remember, the left side shoots right-footed, and the right side shoots left-footed.

- Players should switch lines after they shoot.

Note: *Your players should use only one push to accelerate to the next set of cones. Players should dribble with their heads slightly up, not looking straight down at the ball. Make sure that the person who is receiving the ball is yelling and demanding the ball. Aim to make the players work to score a certain number of goals in a specific time (or over three laps.) Between sets, praise the players for what they did well and constructively correct any mistakes.*

As you can see, this is great technical practice. It requires quick 30-second water breaks to ensure that everything is completed on time. **I recommend setting up the next drill before the previous one is completed if you have enough space and cones to do this.** Otherwise, just set up enough of the drill to demonstrate what needs to be done, then have your players start and quickly set up the rest of the drill. Planning predetermined practices to focus on the necessary areas for improvement will ensure that all your training time is used wisely.

If you are looking for drills with specific coaching points to use in practices that will increase your player's skills, then grab a copy of the *Understand Soccer* series book, *Soccer Drills*. You can also download the free two-page summary, which includes a print-ready version of this one-hour practice at: UnderstandSoccer.com/free-printout

Chapter 9

Rondos

There are hundreds of different things that coaches can focus on with their team during practices. However, the trick is to apply the 80/20 principle when determining what a practice should include. Specifically, the 80/20 principle states that 80% of your beneficial coaching results will come from only 20% of the things that you teach to/work on with your team. This concept is further discussed in the *Understand Soccer* series book, *Soccer Mindset*.

With the 80/20 principle in mind, a key part of an optimized team practice that gives outsized benefits is the "Rondo." A Rondo is a training game similar to "Keep-Away," wherein one group of players must maintain possession of the ball by passing it around players on the opposing side. This game can be played with as little as three players, and there is no maximum number of players. **Rondos train your team to work together, pass in tight spaces, avoid holding onto the ball for too long, and make decisions quickly.**

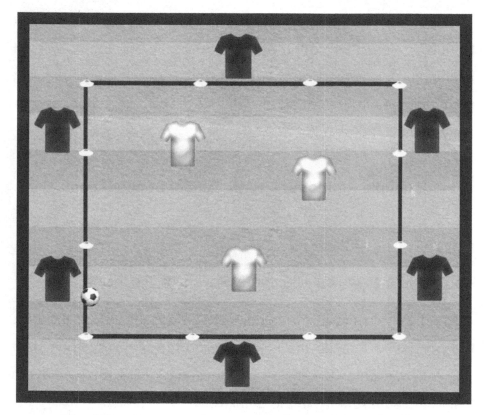

The following are recommendations when using the Rondo:

- **Fewer players are often better.** Form multiple groups of Rondos simultaneously so that more players will be in possession of the ball and improving their skills. An 11v11 Rondo will not help your players as much as a 6v3 Rondo.
- **Create a small area for the Rondo to take place in.** The key target with a Rondo is to make your team more comfortable with playing the ball when they are pressured and decreasing their reaction time for decision-making.

- **Make the Rondo age-specific.** Having a super-complex Rondo, or one in which the players must play one-touch, will not be helpful for a team of seven-year-olds. Conversely, allowing many touches in a huge space will not make high school soccer players much better, either.

Example Rondo for a High School Soccer Team:

- 15-yard x 15-yard box

- Six players on the outside, three players on the inside

- When the players in the middle obtain possession of the ball, the person who made the mistake, and the player to their right and left, will enter the inside of the square. The three players inside the square will join the outside.

Rondo Coaching Tips:

- As your team becomes better at Rondos, you can make the box smaller or limit the number of touches to two or one. This will improve their passing and receiving skills. The Rondo relates to most game situations (except for shooting.) This will result in a game-like training session for your team.

- To teach transitioning from offense to defense after possession is lost, you can go from allowing the players on the inside to walk to their positions on the outside of the square to a more game-like approach, wherein the players must immediately transition when possession changes. This will force players to develop their transitional awareness and mindset, which will in turn keep them from being caught off-guard.

- Create triangle shapes and teach your players how to move so that the player passing the ball will always have two teammates open as targets.

In conclusion, the Rondo is a must for every coach and can even be a terrific warm-up for players to engage in prior to the start of a game. Rondos are used by many powerhouse clubs, such as Liverpool, Barcelona, Ajax, Bayern Munich, and Manchester City. Even the Dutch player and former coach of Barcelona, Johan Cruyff, said, *"Everything that goes on in a match—except shooting—you can do in a rondo. The competitive aspect, fighting to make space, what to do when in possession, and what to do when you have not got the ball, how to play one-touch soccer, how to counteract tight marking, and how to win the ball back."*

YouTube: If you would like to see a video on coaching a rondo, then consider watching the *Understand Soccer* YouTube video: *Rondo Coaching*.

Chapter 10

Ajax Training Method

In international club soccer, the biggest non-national teams play each other over the course of a season and in tournaments to determine the best teams in the world. Examples of club teams are Real Madrid, Paris Saint-Germain, Manchester United, Juventus, River Plate, Bayern Munich, etc.

Clubs have two traditional ways of obtaining good players: (1) The clubs listed in the previous paragraph tend to purchase their players for large sums of money; (2) The other type of club takes young talent and trains them to become the world's top performers. Often, the trained players become so good that the club sells them for large sums of money to teams that are willing to pay.

One of the best examples of a club falling into the latter category is Ajax, a team from the Netherlands. This club is constantly advancing in international competitions because of their educational programs for young athletes, *not* by purchasing superstar players. This speaks volumes about their training methodologies. A few of the top names from within their ranks who have trained from a young age are Johan Cruyff, Christian

Eriksen, Wesley Sneijder, and Dennis Bergkamp. Zlatan Ibrahimović and Luis Suárez also played for Ajax.

One of the biggest underlying decisions that impacts their training is their focus on age-specific soccer skills. Players who are 12 years old and younger focus mostly on their technique with the ball. This means they are working on shooting and finishing, passing and receiving with proper form, heading the ball, and learning various foot skills and the best forms of dribbling. The logic behind this is that these players will play in many systems over the course of their career. Therefore, it is best to focus on building the player, so they can easily adapt to any coaching system. This style of training ensures that they take more touches with the ball than nearly all other players their age. More deliberate touches will quickly raise their confidence, thereby allowing them to become effective soccer players who can play on the game's biggest stages.

For players between the ages of 12 years old and 15 years old, the club directs their attention towards working as a team and being comfortable with building a play by passing the ball. Granted, this does not mean that 12-year-olds and younger players never pass the ball, nor does it mean that the 12-15-year-old players never focus on shooting and foot skills. It merely places the emphasis on one or the other during practices, without entirely cutting out the other important areas of soccer.

Finally, 15-year-olds and older players change their focus to the tactical progression of the team's playstyle. This age group focuses on where each player fits into the team's overarching theme. Ajax has found this to be an appropriate time to increase their strength training, as well.

As a whole, this is a sound system for a club. Granted, you may coach only one age group. But pushing to prioritize certain types of training over different periods of a soccer player's career will turn your club into a premier organization that players seek to join. Yes, this will take coordination with club directors and other coaches, but it is important to understand. Focusing only on foot skills with 18-year-olds and focusing only on team tactics with eight-year-olds makes little sense. Therefore, the appropriate training for each player will be highly impacted by their age.

YouTube: If you would like to see a video on the Ajax Training Method, then consider watching the *Understand Soccer* YouTube video: *Ajax Training Method*.

Chapter 11

The Six-Second Defense

There are two phases of defense: (1) the transition to defense, and (2) being on the defense. According to professional football coach and former player Pep Guardiola, one of the most successful coaches in the world, **Recoveries during the transition to defense are crucial because the best time to regain possession is within the six seconds after the ball was stolen**. Recovering the ball with a six-second burst of high-intensity pressing is also known as "Gegenpressing" or "counter-pressing."

Often, a turnover by your team occurs in the other team's half, so the press is performed by the forwards and midfielders. When forwards and midfielders press the other team for the ball, it is considered to be "high-pressing" and doing it throughout the game will take considerable energy away from the forwards and midfielders who are responsible for scoring. This is why Pep Guardiola and Jürgen Klopp tell their players to counter-press for roughly six seconds, and then assume a standard defensive formation that takes less energy. **This approach requires all the players nearest the ball to rush towards the individual in possession, while the rest of the team moves closer together in a tighter defensive formation.**

The close players shut down passing lanes and attempt to force an immediate mistake. If no error occurs, then the tight positioning is the basis for a tremendous defensive formation. Notice in the below images how the "O" team's defense becomes compacted towards the middle of the field when possession is lost, while ensuring that the opposing player "X" with the ball has no passing lanes open.

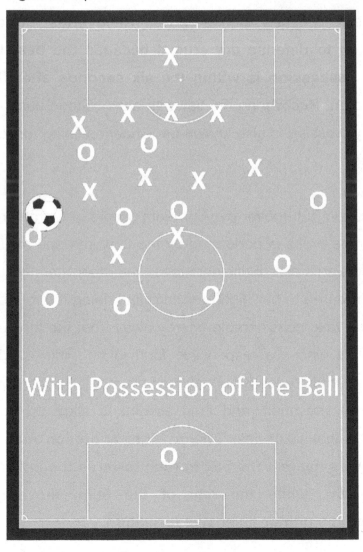

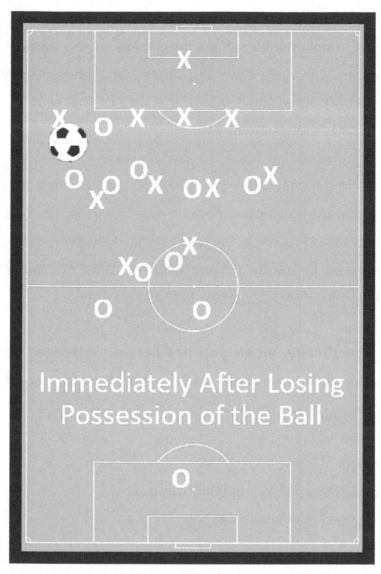

Immediately After Losing
Possession of the Ball

For the six-second defense to be effective, each player must do their part. Pep Guardiola even sold the high-profile players Zlatan Ibrahimović and Yaya Touré because they did not want to be responsible for intense pressing. Counter-pressing is tiring when a loss of possession means the five players nearest the ball need to make 5-10-yard sprints to win the ball back and eliminate passing lanes. However, if this strategy is implemented at the beginning of the season, then your players will likely have the fitness and energy needed to handle counter-pressing towards the end of the season, when games tend to matter the most.

As mentioned, the six seconds after a ball is lost is instrumental in regaining control. In this instance, the trigger for counter-pressing is when the ball is lost. However, this can be coached a bit further for players who are more mentally mature and can comprehend and execute the team play.

Specifically, when you are playing defense, you can coach your team to counter-press with other triggers, like:

- Slow pass
- Bad touch
- Player with the ball facing their own goal
- Off-balanced player with the ball

But remember, this is only effective as a team tactic, so each player needs to know your team's triggers to overwhelm the opposing player with the ball, while providing your defensive players with enough time to regain their shape. This type of triggered pressing resulted in Germany winning the World Cup in

2014 and the German club team Bayern Munich winning the UEFA Champions League in 2013.

YouTube: If you would like to see a video on Gegenpressing, then consider watching the *Understand Soccer* YouTube video: *Counter Pressing - How to Coach the Six-Second Defense*.

Section 3
Formations

Chapter 12

4-4-2 Formation

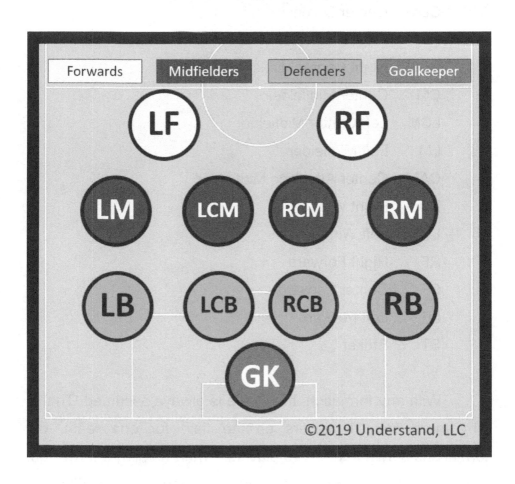

GK   Goalkeeper

RB   Right Back

RCB   Right Center Back

CB   Center Back

LCB   Left Center Back

LB	Left Back
RWB	Right Wing Back
LWB	Left Wing Back
CDM	Center Defensive Midfielder
RM	Right Midfielder
RCM	Right Center Midfielder
CM	Center Midfielder
LCM	Left Center Midfielder
LM	Left Midfielder
CAM	Center Attacking Midfielder
RW	Right Winger
LW	Left Winger
RF	Right Forward
CF	Center Forward
LF	Left Forward
ST	Striker

With any formation, the goalie is always assumed. That is why there are 11 players on the field for one team, but formations only add up to 10 players. When naming a formation, the number of defenders comes first, followed by the midfielders, and then the forwards. In this and upcoming chapters, the "Big 3" and most other formations will be discussed to help determine which formation is best for your team. **You will also learn that each formation is stronger against some formations and weaker against others**. However, a well-selected formation alone cannot compensate for a team that cannot pass, shoot with accuracy, has minimal skill with the ball, and does not defend properly. Dynamic players who can change as needed are best for any formation, but a well-selected formation with the players' abilities in mind will reap the biggest results. Therefore, a good coach should consider their team's skills and deficiencies when determining the best formation.

The standard formation for most youth teams with new coaches, and many professional-level English teams, is the 4-4-2 formation. Some club teams shy away from this formation because many top directors see this as a formation used by teams who are unconvinced of their players' abilities and their coaching staff's skills. This formation is easy to teach at any level and does not involve advanced offensive game planning.

This formation uses four defenders, four midfielders, and two forwards. **The most common variation of the 4-4-2 is where the four midfielders are in a diamond formation.** This formation has one center attacking midfielder, and one center defensive/holding midfielder. Also, you may find the forwards stacked, instead of side-by-side. The topmost forward would act as the striker, and the forward between the striker and center attacking midfielder would act as the center forward.

The other most common variation of this formation is the 4-1-3-2, which uses a holding/defensive center midfielder, and three other midfielders/wingers who play higher up the field.

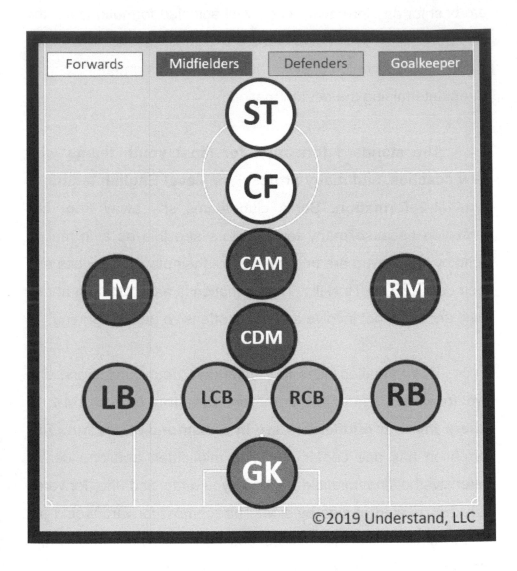

Forwards | Midfielders | Defenders | Goalkeeper

ST
CF
CAM
LM   RM
CDM
LB   LCB   RCB   RB
GK

©2019 Understand, LLC

Strengths

This balanced formation provides enough players to attack and defend. This type of formation ensures that a team can easily work the ball from the defense to the midfield and (usually) maintain continuous possession. **Many coaches prefer this formation because it is the easiest to teach, and one of the simplest for players to understand.**

This formation is great when a team does not have many all-star-caliber players who can carry the scoring responsibilities by themselves. **Furthermore, this formation provides width in the midfield, and enough defense to slow the opposition's progress both up the flanks and the center of the field.** Conversely, the 4-4-2 is great for teams with outside midfielders or wing backs who excel at the crossing the ball into the box towards forwards/strikers, as well as midfielders who excel at scoring from crosses. This formation has an advantage in the midfield over teams playing a 4-3-3.

Weaknesses

This formation heavily relies on good forwards and strikers who can dribble past and possess the ball effectively against the opposing defenders. Teams who implement this formation often only score a couple of goals per game. This formation does not have enough forwards/strikers to overcome an opposing team using the 5-4-1.

Without proper coaching, the outside midfielders may act like wingers and not track back well enough on defense. **Conversely, the outside midfielder may be so concerned with marking the opposing player in their position that they focus more on defense than producing goals.** This type of player will spend their energy tracking back and making sure that their opponent never scores, but it will be the expense of creating scoring opportunities themselves. Finally, the 4-4-2 has been around for years, so it is predictable. Therefore, the other team will usually be familiar with ways to beat and defend against it.

Notable Teams That Have Used the 4-4-2 Formation

Arsenal's "Invincibles" team of 2003/04 achieved great success using the 4-4-2. This is the only English Premier League team in the modern era to go an entire 38-match season without losing a game.

The Manchester United team of 1998/99 used this formation to win the treble under Sir Alex Ferguson. Sir Alex Ferguson's soccer mind resulted in many variations of the 4-4-2 to confuse the opposition, but the general formation largely remained the same.

Chapter 13

5-4-1 Formation

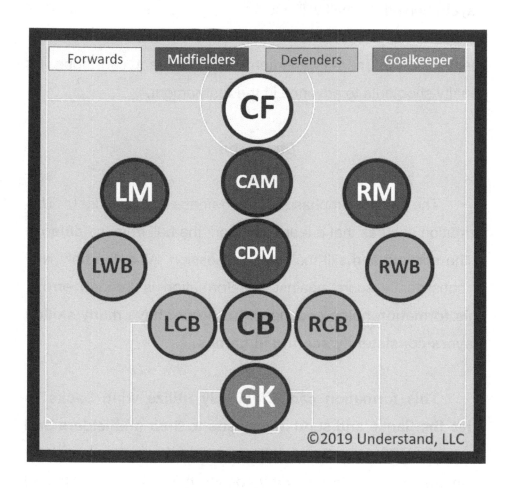

©2019 Understand, LLC

This formation features five defenders, four midfielders, and one forward. **The 5-4-1 is a very defensive formation.** 10 players out of the team's 11 will have defensive responsibilities, so this formation is for teams with a lot of defenders who care most about keeping the other team off the stat sheet. Often, teams with less skilled players will use this formation. Also, this formation is used by tiny nations who do not have the same scoring abilities as the world soccer powerhouses. Having many players behind the ball will ensure many 0-0 ties or 1-0 victories for the team. This formation is effective when playing more talented teams in a tournament, as the team can hope for penalty shootouts to advance in the tournament.

Strengths

The 5-4-1 emphasizes a defense-first mindset. This formation ensures that a team can work the ball from the defense to the midfield and still maintain possession. Also, the only way to consistently score against this formation is through errors. **This formation helps coaches who do not have many skilled players consistently scoring in games.**

This formation can effectively utilize wing backs to drive the flanks and send in crosses to their midfielders and forward. With so many defenders, this team can quickly counterattack the other team by booting the ball up the field and letting their dominant center forward go to work.

Finally, a 5-4-1 has a defensive advantage over teams that play a 4-4-2.

Weaknesses

This formation makes it difficult for the other team to score, but also **makes it difficult for your own team to score**. Most players will be too deep in defensive positions to create chances or support the lonely center forward while attacking. Also, because there is little opportunity for players on the team to score, this formation is often disliked by many midfielders and forwards because they want to score goals, and this formation does not cater to that.

This lack of goal production can quickly reduce the spirits of many midfielders and forwards, who may feel like they are not making a meaningful impact on the team. This formation requires teamwork and discipline because incorrect moves can open passing lanes and allow the other team to score. Also, this formation relies heavily on an all-star center forward, who can control the ball and score—even with multiple people covering them.

Finally, this formation does not have enough forwards/strikers to keep pace by scoring enough goals to keep up with a team using a 4-3-3.

Notable Teams That Have Used the 5-4-1 Formation

The Chelsea team of the 2004/05 season earned the most points in an English Premier League season up to that point in time. This team was coached by José Mourinho and featured Didier Drogba as a pivotal center forward. He was required to score and hold the ball for teammates. Without a great point-man, this formation is not as effective.

In the 2014 World Cup, the small island nation of Costa Rica won their group against the huge soccer nations of Uruguay, Italy, and England. Their manager, Jorge Pinto, realized his team lacked the skills and abilities of their opponents, so they wanted to "park the bus" in front of their net and counterattack when they dispossessed the other team. Costa Rica was knocked out of the quarterfinal by penalty kicks but only gave up one goal during their entire campaign.

Chapter 14

4-3-3 Formation

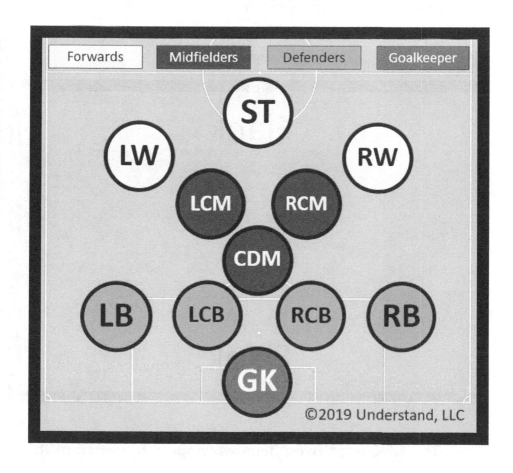

Forwards Midfielders Defenders Goalkeeper

ST
LW   RW
LCM   RCM
CDM
LB   LCB   RCB   RB
GK

©2019 Understand, LLC

This formation features four defenders, three midfielders, and three forwards. **The 4-3-3 formation is all about placing a strong emphasis on scoring many goals in each game.** Late in games, when a team is down by a goal or two, the coach will often change the formation to a 4-3-3 to increase the chance of producing a goal at the expense of giving up a midfield player.

This is because, in most circumstances, it does not matter how many goals a team loses by. In the 4-3-3, the midfield is located more centrally and works to clog up the midfield and dispossess the other team. Once possession is won, the ball is played to the wings and carried up the field's flanks.

The **4-3-3 uses two offensive wingers to transport the ball up the flanks and cross it into the box** or to cut in and strike it like an inverted winger.

The 4-3-3 formation has had a tremendous impact in Spanish soccer—to no one's surprise—because of the talent hotbed that Spain has become for soccer players. A common variation of the 4-3-3 is the 4-3-2-1.

If any these player positions seem a bit confusing, then consider grabbing a copy of the *Understand Soccer* series book, *Soccer Positions*, to fully understand each major position in soccer and the role, skills needed, and number associated with each position.

Strengths

The basic 4-3-3 formation is the ultimate attacking formation of the "Big 3." This formation often has a high defensive line in which the whole defense pushes up the field to be readily available if the other team obtains possession of the ball, as well as to use the offside trap against the opposing team. If you have two very fit wingers, then the 4-3-3 formation can become a 4-5-1 formation, based on the flow of the game— especially when possession is lost.

The 4-3-3 generally uses three central midfielders, who aim to dominate the center of the pitch and force the opposing team to move the ball up the sides of the field. This formation works best with technically strong players who can maintain possession of the ball. Furthermore, the positioning itself makes maintaining possession easier by featuring many passing angles and plenty of offensive players ready to receive the ball. Because the 4-3-3 has more forwards than the formations discussed in previous chapters, the three attacking players are expected to press the other team's defense when the opposing team has the ball. A defensive turnover by the other team will make it easy for the attackers to score because there will be few opposing players to beat. Also, because the flanks of the field are so open, the outside defensive backs will often function more like wing backs and carry the ball up the wings of the field. Finally, a 4-3-3 has an offensive player advantage over teams playing a 5-4-1.

Weaknesses

The 4-3-3 may be an unreasonable formation for a team that does not have three players who can consistently score. Using a 4-3-3 requires a team's forwards to work well together, and each offensive player must contribute in terms of goals and assists. Often, because this formation has many offensive players, one of the midfielders will need to play like a center defensive midfielder (i.e., holding midfielder) to help stop the other team from quickly moving the ball up the field after they gain possession of it.

Furthermore, having six players with some offensive responsibilities may result in situations where **the other team**

can counterattack and quickly pass by six players seemingly at once. Because many midfielders will be centrally located, the wings/flanks of the field will often be wide-open and easy to carry the ball into.

The trick to a successful 4-3-3 formation occurs when the team using the 4-3-3 gains possession. Without the ball, the players should be compact, but when possession is gained, the entire team must work to spread out, both in terms of width and depth, across the field.

Additionally, the 4-3-3 formation provides many gaps, which an opposing team with good passing abilities can exploit to quickly move the ball from a defender to a midfielder, and then to a forward. **Conversely, because the team using the 4-3-3 tends to be compacted towards the middle of the field, the opposition can easily play the ball from one side of the field to the other. This will allow them to begin attacking from the opposite side of the field, which will have no wide players to prevent this from occurring.** Finally, this formation does not have enough midfielders when matched against a 4-4-2.

Notable Teams That Have Used the 4-3-3 Formation

The 2014/15 Barcelona team won the treble by winning La Liga, the Copa del Rey, and the Champions League titles. Barcelona effectively used this system under their coach, Luis Enrique, because they had the lineup of a generation. With Messi, Suarez, and Neymar as attacking players, and Rakitić, Sergio, and Roberto as the midfield, this team was formed with the sole purpose of moving the ball to the three attackers, known as "MSN." MSN netted 122 goals, the most in a season during all competitions for an offensive trio in Spanish soccer history.

The 2008-2012 Spanish national team implemented the 4-3-3 as a possession-oriented formation. They became known for their Tiki-taka style of passing (i.e., one-or-two-touch passing) to wear down opponents, so the other team would go for stretches of up to 10 minutes without even touching the ball. Forcing the other team to constantly play defense and chase the ball allowed the Spanish national team to win the Euro 2008, the 2010 World Cup, and the Euro 2012.

Chapter 15

Other Formations

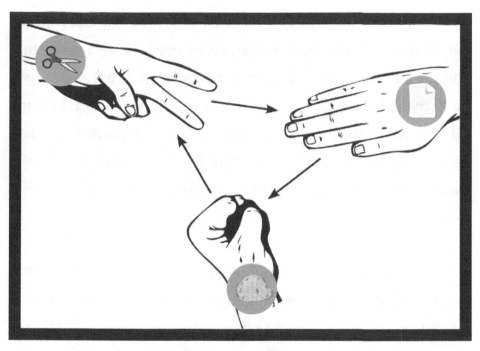

For the formations already mentioned, **think of the "Big 3" formations (e.g., 4-4-2, 5-4-1, and 4-3-3) as "Rock, Paper, Scissors."** Each formation has advantages over another and is disadvantaged by another. The 4-4-2 provides an advantage over the 4-3-3 because the 4-4-2's four midfielders can overwhelm the other team's three midfielders. The 4-3-3 provides an advantage over the 5-4-1 because having so many attacking players provides a constant barrage against a team that is very defensive-minded. The 5-4-1 provides a defensive advantage over the 4-4-2 because the attacking forces are often overwhelmed by the number of defending players.

A good coach will assess their players' skills and team's abilities against the opposing teams. **A knowledgeable coach will know that forcing a preferred formation on a team that cannot handle it is a recipe for disaster. A great coach will pick their formation based on their players, and not the other way around.** Teams with very skilled players typically have more forwards and favor the 4-3-3, whereas teams with less technical skills but more good defenders will benefit from a 5-4-1.

As we have discussed in the past few chapters, the 4-4-2, 5-4-1, and 4-3-3 are considered by many to be the "Big 3" formations. However, based on your team's skillset, a different formation may be better. The remaining formations are listed below, in order of most defensive to most offensive:

Most Defensive: 5-3-2
4-2-3-1 (like a 4-5-1)
3-2-3-2 (like a 3-5-2)
3-4-3
4-2-4
3-3-4
W-M (like a 3-2-5)

2-3-5

1-2-7

Most Offensive: Dutch Total Football

Note: Please keep in mind that there are many variations of each of these. You may have heard of or read about some of them. Therefore, this order is not definite; it only acts as a guide to aid in selecting a formation for your team.

5-3-2

The 5-3-2 is a defensive-oriented formation, like the 5-4-1. However, this formation adds another forward to help score. This formation often has three midfield players centrally located. The ball is typically moved up the center of the field. A variation of this formation involves a sweeper behind the line of four defenders. **This formation requires midfielders and forwards who are skilled at receiving the ball and using foot skills to beat defenders.** This formation is strong in the middle of the field but lacks the width needed in the flanks. Therefore, opposing teams will find many opportunities to cross the ball into the box from wide positions on the field. To counteract excessive amounts of crosses, often the rightmost and leftmost defenders will defend farther up the field and work the ball up the sides of the field to help the midfielders and forwards when their team has possession.

The Italian "catenaccio" is a defensive variation of this formation, with the innovation of using a sweeper (also known as a "libero" or "free man.") The four main defenders had the task of strictly man-marking the opposition's forwards in a time when the opposition likely had at least four forwards. The sweeper acted as a layer of additional defense when the other team had the ball.

4-2-3-1

The 4-2-3-1 is like a 4-5-1 in that there are two holding midfielders, and three midfielders who are focused primarily on helping the team score. **The holding midfielders can win the ball and significantly limit the other team's ability to move the ball through the middle of the field. A great holding midfielder can be a phenomenal passer with great accuracy and wonderful vision to pass to attacking midfielders, wingers, forwards, and strikers, who can in turn receive the ball and travel behind the opposition's back line.**

The 4-2-3-1 has many centrally located players. Therefore, one of its greatest weaknesses is its lack of width to help carry the ball up the sides of the pitch.

3-2-3-2

The 3-2-3-2 is like a 3-5-2 in that there are five midfielders. This formation (and the others discussed so far in this chapter) all lack width in the midfield. **Often, these centrally oriented formations will be used by coaches with players who are talented with the ball at their feet (i.e., players with good foot skills, as well as passing and receiving abilities.)** On one hand, staying centrally located makes it easier for the opposition to attack in the flanks. On the other hand, clogging up the middle ensures that opposing teams with very skilled players cannot effectively move the ball through the most dangerous part of the field, the middle.

3-4-3

The 3-4-3 is a favorite of many youth teams, including the Dutch powerhouse club, Ajax. As mentioned previously, the Ajax club team cares deeply about developing their talent from a young age. As such, they care more about focusing on each player's skills and abilities than on which formation the players use. Specifically, Ajax is not as concerned with wins and losses in their youth programs as they are with developing each player in the system.

Personally, this formation really resonates with me because having only three defenders will ensure many 1v1 situations against attacking players on the opposing team. This in turn greatly increases the abilities of the defenders, who are required to read the field from a young age and know when to dive in for the ball and when to slow the attacker and wait for support.

Next, having four midfielders and three forwards will help overwhelm the other team's defense. Having many players attacking means the offense will have more touches on the ball. More touches on the ball will ensure that players gain additional experience quicker. **Because there are usually not enough defenders on the opposing side to control the 3-4-3, the attacking players will become more comfortable working with their teammates and improving their 1v1 foot skills, and they will appreciate having more chances to score.** While this formation often allows many goals to be scored against it, it also helps improve each player's abilities much faster than playing a 4-4-2 or a 5-4-1 would.

4-2-4

The 4-2-4 is a largely unused formation involving an overpowered offense, a strong defense, and large gaps in the middle of the field. The premise behind this formation is to have many attacking players (i.e., the four forwards) and many defending players (i.e., the four defenders). Since scoring and preventing the other team from scoring are the two most important objectives of most teams, this formation places players in positions to fulfill those objectives. Often, the two midfielders will be centrally located and act as holding/defensive midfielders to stop the other team's progress up the field and deliver the ball back to their forwards.

The 1970 Brazilian World Cup team won the tournament because of this formation, as well as their talented forwards who made this system effective.

3-3-4

This formation focuses on using a midfield playmaker to direct most of the attacking plays with laser-like passes and outstanding vision of the field. In the 1950s and 1960s, this was the most common formation, after the WM formation. This formation saw a small resurgence when Antonio Conte implemented it to win the Serie A with Juventus—though it could be argued that it may not have been the formation that won the Italian league, as Juventus had the best players of any team in Italy at the time. Also, Conte used this formation for the offense at Chelsea, but it resembled more of a 3-4-3 when his team was on defense.

W-M

The W-M formation essentially involves five forwards and five defenders. However, two of the forwards are on the inside right and inside left and at times double as attacking center midfielders. Also, two of the defenders act more like holding/defensive center midfielders, whose job is to stop the other team from passing and dribbling up the field.

A variation of this is the Hungarian M–U formation, in which the center forward will drop deep into the midfield to pull the center back out of position, similar to the role of the False Nine.

Therefore, it would be justifiable to call the W-M formation a kind of 3-2-5—or even a distant variation of a 3-4-3. As with any formation, how the players react to it and move will reveal its pros and cons.

In 1925, the offside rule changed the number of players needed between each team and their goal from three down to two. This change prompted the English Premier League team, Arsenal, to use the WM formation by adding more defenders to the backfield to help combat the change in rules.

2-3-5

The 2-3-5 is also known as the "inverted pyramid." Once the soccer world began to realize that passing was a more effective way to move the ball, the 2-3-5 became the standard formation. Similar to the W-M, this offense-minded formation was a result of time and what spectators considered to be a "good soccer game," which in turn influenced ticket purchases.

The 2-3-5 has two central defenders, three midfielders, and five forwards. The forwards are a left winger, an inside left, a center forward, an inside right, and a right winger.

1–2–7

This was the first standard formation used by soccer teams in England. **Prior to this formation, soccer predominately involved dribbling the ball, with passing as a last resort.** This concept was rooted in England during the 1800s and was similar to the other English sport of rugby. The single defender was known as the three-quarter-back. The two midfielders used passing to direct their team's numerous offensive players. The seven forwards were split into four wingers and three center forwards. The wingers' main task was to use their pace to collect long balls sent forward by the half-backs and three-quarter-backs, whereas the center forwards were charged with taking short passes from the wingers and were responsible for much of the goal-scoring.

Dutch Total Football

This system relied on versatile players who could attack and defend, depending on the game situation. This formation is listed as the most offensive because each player could attack. The two biggest criticisms about it were that it never won a major trophy for the Netherlands, and it required each player to be a jack of all trades, which meant they would be a master of none. Johan Cruyff, one of the best to ever play the game, was the Captain of the Dutch National Team and could effectively play in each outfield position. He was a major reason for Dutch Total Football's relative success during his career for his country.

If you look at the formations from the top of the list to the bottom, you will initially see more present-day formations with many defenders. As you travel down the list, you will notice the formations are from older generations and are considerably more offensive-minded. As you can see by the descriptions of the lesser-used formations, soccer started off as a much more offense-oriented sport. **It took almost a century for the soccer community to realize that having less than four forwards was ideal to ensure a stable defense.**

In the early days, soccer was played to win just as much as it was to be entertaining for the fans. Therefore, a formation with five attacking players on both sides resulted in many games with upwards of eight goals scored per match. During soccer's infancy, spectators were much more likely to pay for tickets when the score line included many goals, as opposed to the more familiar score lines of 1-0 for today's modern game. Soccer did not transition into a defense-first mindset for most teams until smaller nations with less talented players began to place more players in defensive positions to compete with larger nations. After all, there is some truth to the saying, "Defense wins championships."

Additionally, as with many formations mentioned in this chapter, the horizontal lines of the Big 3 formations are disappearing. Specifically, in the old days, there were three distinct lines of players (i.e., forwards, midfielders, and defenders), but this is becoming a thing of the past. Many modern coaches use formations that allow their players to travel between the lines, where there is considerably more space. Any of the formations in this chapter involving four numbers (e.g., the 4-1-3-2) aim to help break the three-horizontal-line mold of the Big 3 formations by giving each player on a team a more specific role on the field. In the modern soccer game, in which players' skillsets are continually becoming more advanced, using a formation that highlights each player's abilities will help ensure continued success.

Finally, understand that teams may have different formations when they are playing offense versus defense. For the most part, the positions will stay the same for nearly all players—except for one or two, who will have increased responsibilities. **These increased responsibilities are normally given to players with considerable stamina and endurance.** For example, a team attacking with a 4-3-3 formation may have a coach who asks one or both wingers to track back and create either a 4-4-2 or a 4-5-1 when their team no longer has possession of the ball.

However, a coach must recognize that having double the responsibilities is energy-consuming for a player and will require great tactical knowledge of when to travel forward versus when to hold back.

Afterword

To be a great coach, you must continue to learn, grow, and find what works best for you and your team. As the former U.S. President Harry S. Truman stated, "**Leaders are readers**." Therefore, do not stop improving your soccer knowledge, as there is a considerable amount to learn for every coach, trainer, parent, and player. You have taken the time to read this book, so you have already revealed that you likely care more and are more committed than most other coaches. Therefore, I applaud you for your efforts and want to let you know that they have not gone unnoticed.

Take the information revealed in this book to the field immediately to impact your team's game. It is not enough just to read the information; you must immediately apply it. **The trick to improvement and positive change is massive action.** Therefore, there is no better time than the present to improve your team.

If you enjoyed this book, then please leave a review on Amazon to let me know. If you learned from this book, then consider ordering a copy of the *Understand Soccer* series books *Soccer Positions* and *Soccer Dribbling & Foot Skills* to continue advancing your knowledge of this "beautiful game."

WAIT!

Wouldn't it be nice to have the one-hour practice discussed in this book, as well as a parent questionnaire, on an easy two-page printout to take to the field? Well, here is your chance!

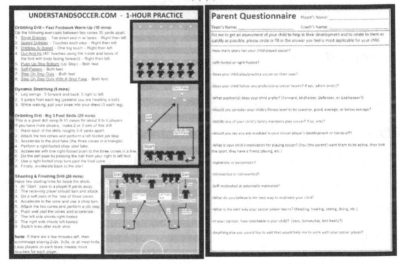

Go to this Link for an **Instant** Two-Page Printout:
UnderstandSoccer.com/free-printout

These FREE guides are simply a thank you for purchasing this book. This two-page printout will ensure that you are ready for practice, and the accompanying questionnaire will gauge the interest of your players and their parents.

About the Author

There he was—a soccer player who had difficulties scoring. He wanted to be the best on the field but lacked the confidence and knowledge to make his goal a reality. Every day, he dreamed about improving, but the average coaching he received, combined with his lack of knowledge, only left him feeling alone and unable to attain his goal. He was a quiet player, and his performance often went unnoticed.

This all changed after his junior year on the varsity soccer team of one of the largest high schools in the state. During the team and parent banquet at the end of the season, his coach decided to say something nice about each player. When it was his turn to receive praise, the only thing that could be said was that he had scored two goals that season—even though they were against a lousy team, so they didn't really count. It was a very painful statement that after the 20+ game season, all that could be said of his efforts were two goals that didn't count. One of his greatest fears came true; he was called out in front of his family and friends.

Since that moment, he was forever changed. He got serious. With a new soccer mentor, he focused on training to obtain the necessary skills, build his confidence, and become the goal-scorer that he'd always dreamed of being. The next season, after just a few months, he found himself moved up to the starting position of center midfielder and scored his first goal of the 26-game season in only the third game.

He continued with additional training led by a proven goal-scorer to build his knowledge. Fast-forward to the present day, and, as a result of the work he put in, and his focus on the necessary skills, he figured out how to become a goal-scorer who averages about two goals and an assist per game—all because he increased his understanding of how to play soccer. With the help of a soccer mentor, he took his game from being a bench-warmer who got called out in front of everybody to becoming the most confident player on the field.

Currently, he is a soccer trainer in Michigan, working for Next Level Training. He advanced through their rigorous program as a soccer player and was hired as a trainer. This program has allowed him to guide world-class soccer players for over a decade. He trains soccer players in formats ranging from one-hour classes to weeklong camps, and he instructs classes of all sizes, from groups of 30 soccer players all the way down to working one-on-one with individuals who want to play for the United States National Team.

If you enjoyed this book, then please leave a review.

Additional Books by Dylan Joseph Available on Amazon:

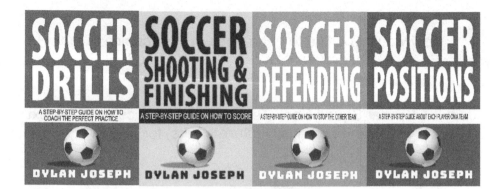

Soccer Drills: A Step-by-Step Guide on How to Coach the Perfect Practice

Soccer Shooting & Finishing: A Step-by-Step Guide on How to Score

Soccer Defending: A Step-by-Step Guide on How to Stop the Other Team

Soccer Positions: A-Step-by-Step Guide about Each Player on a Team

Free Book!

How would you like to get a book of your choice in the *Understand Soccer* series for free?

Join the Soccer Squad Book Team today and receive your next book (and potentially future books) for FREE.

Signing up is easy and does not cost anything.

Check out this website for more information:

UnderstandSoccer.com/soccer-squad-book-team

Thank You for Reading!

Dear Reader,

I hope you enjoyed and learned from *Soccer Coaching: A Step-by-Step Guide on How to Lead Your Players, Manage Parents, and Select the Best Formation.* I enjoyed writing these steps and tips to help you improve your confidence, your player's skills, and your communication with their parents.

As an author, I love feedback. Candidly, you are the reason that I wrote this book and plan to write more. Therefore, I'd love to hear from you. Tell me what you liked, what you loved, and what can be improved. Visit UnderstandSoccer.com and scroll to the bottom of the homepage to leave me a message in the contact section or email me directly at:

Dylan@UnderstandSoccer.com

Finally, I need to ask a favor: **I'd love and appreciate a review.** As you likely know, reviews are a key part of my process to see whether you enjoyed my book. Your reviews allow me to write more books. Please take two minutes to leave a review on Amazon.com at:

https://www.amazon.com/gp/product-review/1949511154

In gratitude,

Dylan Joseph

Glossary

10 & 4 - The defensive position where your feet represent hands on a clock. Use this positioning when you want to push the attacking player to their left foot.

4-3-3 Formation - Four defenders, three midfielders, and three forwards. An offensive formation.

4-4-2 Formation - Four defenders, four midfielders, and two forwards. A standard and balanced formation.

50-50 - When a ball is passed into pressure or cleared up the field, and your teammate and a player on the opposing team each have an equal (i.e., 50%) chance of taking possession of the ball.

5-4-1 Formation (i.e., "Low Block") - Five defenders, four midfielders, and one forward. A defensive formation.

8 & 2 - The defensive position where your feet represent hands on a clock. Use this positioning when you want to push the attacking player to their right foot.

80/20 Principle - 80% of your results come from only 20% of your actions.

Back Line - The defenders on a soccer team forming the line in front of the goalkeeper.

Ball Hawk - Someone usually close to the ball, in the right place at the right time, and a person who specializes in scoring rebounds.

Bat - The bone (i.e., hardest portion) of your foot.

Behind the Ball - When a player is between the ball and the net.

Bent/Curved Shot - A shot that spins and curves as it goes towards the net. This shot is used when you need to shoot around defenders or goalkeepers. Use the bone of your foot to strike the ball. Instead of following through the ball with your entire body, just follow through with your leg and cross your legs after shooting the ball.

Bicycle Kick (i.e., "Overhead Kick") - where the ball is above you and you jump up and kick the ball over your body while the ball is in the air.

Big 3 Foot Skills - The body feint (jab step), self-pass, and the shot fake.

Big 3 Formations - 4-4-2, 5-4-1, and 4-3-3 formations.

Block - Deflecting or stopping the shot of an opposing player.

Body Feint (i.e., "Feint," "Fake," "Fake and Take," "Jab Step," or "Shoulder Drop") - When you pretend to push the ball in one direction, but purposely miss, then plant with the same foot and then push the ball in the other direction with the opposite foot.

Broom - In this book, it is the area on your foot towards your toes. There is space in your shoe between your toes where there is a lot more fabric and a lot less bone, which makes it a soft area on your foot, similar to the softness of a broom.

Champions League - A tournament of qualifying teams in Europe held yearly to determine who is considered the world's best club team (the European Champion). Often considered one of the top two trophies that every soccer player dreams of winning (the other being the World Cup).

Chop - This is performed with the outside of your foot. The leg that is cutting the ball must step entirely past the ball. Then, allow the ball to hit that leg/foot, which effectively stops the ball. Having the ball stop next to your foot enables the ball to be pushed in a different direction quickly.

Clearance - Kicking the ball up the field and out of pressure.

Counterattack (i.e., "Fast Break") - When the defending team gains possession of the ball and quickly moves the ball up the field with the objective of taking a quick shot, so few of the other team's players will have time to travel back to defend.

Crossbar Challenge - Played by one or more people where you attempt to hit the crossbar by shooting the ball from the 18-yard box.

Cruyff - Cut the ball while leaving yourself between the defender and the ball. In essence, cut the ball behind your plant leg.

Cut - This is performed with the inside of your foot. The leg that is cutting the ball must step entirely past the ball. Then, allow the ball to hit that leg/foot, which effectively stops the ball. Having the ball stop next to your foot enables the ball to be pushed in a different direction quickly. Additionally, you may cut the ball so that it is immediately moving in the direction that you want to go.

Deliberate Practice - This form of practice is purposeful practice that knows where it is going and how to get there. It is guided by an understanding of what expert performers do to excel. For example, juggling with the tops of your feet towards the toes 30 times in a row to become better at settling the ball out of the air.

Driven Shot (i.e., "Sledgehammer Shot") - A shot struck with the bone of your foot, where you follow through with your entire body without crossing your legs. This is the most powerful type of shot.

Dynamic Stretching - Movement-based stretching that uses the muscles themselves to stretch other muscles (e.g., shaking out your arms and performing leg swings). It is different from traditional "static" stretching because the stretched position is not held.

False Nine - A soccer player positioned as a center forward but plays more like an attacking midfielder to draw defenders out of the back line.

Finishing - The purpose of shooting, which is to score.

Flank - The right or left sides of the field closest to the sidelines.

Flick - When you barely touch the ball when receiving a pass to slightly change its direction as a way to pass it to a teammate.

Formation - The positioning of players on the field assigned by the coach.

Foundations - Passing the ball back and forth from one foot to the other using the inside of your feet.

Gegenpressing (i.e., "Counter-Pressing" or "Six-Second Defense") - High pressure within the first six seconds after losing possession of the ball, while the opponent is not yet set up properly to attack.

Habitual/Regular Practice - The most common form of practice where a person goes through the motions, repeating what they normally do, without being challenged or having a set goal. For example, practicing shooting from the penalty spot for fifth practice in a row.

Half-Volley - Striking the ball just after it hit the ground, but while the ball is still in the air.

High-Pressing - Defending high up the pitch and inside the opposition's half. Forwards are usually the main instigators to defend far away from their own goal.

Holding Midfielder (i.e., "Defensive Midfielder") - A midfielder who sits in front of the back line and protects the center of the field.

Hyped - Promote an idea or action intensively to emphasize its importance or benefits.

Interception - Stepping into a passing lane to dispossess the other team during a pass.

Jockeying - When defending, backpedaling to maintain proper position in relation to the person attacking with the ball. When jockeying, the defender does not dive in for the ball. Instead, they wait for the ideal time to steal the ball or poke it away.

Jump Turn - Instead of pulling the ball back with the bottom of your foot, (i.e., the V-pull-back), stop the ball with the bottom of your foot as you jump past it, landing with both feet at the same time on the other side of the ball, which will allow you to explode away in the direction you came from.

Mindset - The established set of attitudes held by someone.

Moving First Touch (i.e., "Attacking Touch") - Pushing the ball into space with your first touch, which is the opposite of taking a touch where the ball stops underneath you (i.e., at your feet).

Offside - When you pass the ball to a teammate who is past the opposing team's last defender when the kick is initiated. You cannot be offside on a throw-in, or when you are on your own half of the field.

One-Time Shot - When a pass or cross is played to you and your first touch is a shot on net.

Opposite Foot - Your non-dominant foot. Out of your two feet, it is the one that you are not as comfortable using.

Outside of the Foot Shot (i.e., "Trivela") - Shooting with the bone of your foot where your toe is pointed down and in. The ball makes contact with the outside portion/bone of your foot. This shot is useful because it is quicker than a driven shot, it can provide bend like a bent shot, and is more powerful than a pass shot.

Park the Bus - Often, when a team has a lead, a coach will tell all their players to come back and focus almost exclusively on defense to help protect the lead

Pass Fake - Faking a pass. Keep your form the same as when you pass, including: 1) Looking at a teammate before you do a pass fake 2) Raise your passing leg high enough behind your body, so that an opponent believes you are going to kick the ball.

Pass Shot (i.e., "Finesse Shot" or "Instep Drive") - A shot on the net using the inside of your foot to increase your accuracy. However, land past the ball on the follow through to increase the shot's power, similar to a shot taken with the bone of your foot.

Passing Lane - An area on the field where a teammate can pass you the ball directly, while the ball remains on the ground.

Pitch - A soccer field.

Point-Man - Often a tall and strong center forward, capable of winning 50-50 battles when the ball has been cleared up the field. This player's size and/or abilities help them hold off the defenders, thereby allowing other teammates to join the attack and travel into passing lanes.

Purposeful Practice - Setting specific goals for what you want to complete successfully (e.g., "I want to juggle the ball 30 times without letting it hit the ground.")

Rainbow - When you place one foot in front of the ball and the laces of the other foot behind the ball. Pin the ball between your feet and flick the ball up behind your body and over your head.

Recovery - Intercepting a pass shortly after your team was dispossessed.

Roll (i.e., "Rollover") - Using the bottom of the toes of your foot, roll the ball parallel to the defender, crossing your feet when you plant. Then, bring your other foot around to uncross your feet and push the ball forward. The path the ball takes is the shape of an "L."

Rondo - A training game similar to "keep away" where one group of players must maintain possession of the ball by passing it around members of the opposing side.

Sandwich Feedback Technique - Give a compliment, followed by giving feedback with an explanation ended with another compliment.

Scissor - A foot skill where your foot closest to the ball goes around it as you are attacking a defender. Emphasize turning your hips to fake the defender. To easily turn your hips, plant past the ball with the foot that is not going around it so that you can use the momentum of the moving ball to your advantage.

Self-Pass (i.e., "L," "Iniesta," or "La Croqueta") - Passing the ball from one foot to the other while running. Imagine you are doing a roll, but without your foot going on top of the ball. Instead, it is an inside of the foot pass from one foot and an inside of the foot push up the field with the other foot.

Set Piece (i.e., "Dead Ball") - A practiced plan used when the ball goes out of bounds, or a foul is committed to put the ball back into play. The most common set pieces are throw-ins and free kicks.

Shielding - Placing your body between the ball and the defender with your back facing the defender and your arms wide, thereby preventing the defender from traveling to the ball.

Shot Fake - Faking a shot. Make sure your form looks the same as when you shoot, including: 1) Looking at the goal before you do a shot fake 2) Arms out 3) Raise your shooting leg high enough behind your body, so it looks like you will shoot.

Six-Second Defense (i.e., "Gegenpressing" or "Counter-pressing") - High-intensity pressing for the six seconds after losing possession of the ball in order to gain it back before the opposing team is in their attacking positions.

Square to Your Teammate - Pointing your hips at a teammate.

Step-On-Step-Out - To change direction, step on the ball with the bottom of your foot. Then, with the same foot that stepped on the ball, take another step to plant to the side of the ball, so that your other leg can come through and push the ball in a different direction.

Step-Over - When you are next to the ball, and your farthest leg steps over the ball. Your entire body turns, as if you were going in a completely different direction. The step-over is best used along a sideline or with your back facing the direction in which you need to travel (e.g., a forward with the ball who's back is facing the opposing team's net).

Sweeper (i.e., "Libero" or "Free Man") - A defender that has no specific man-marking responsibilities and will often be situated behind their defending teammates to help "sweep up" any balls that travel through the defensive line.

Through Ball/Run - When a pass is played into the space in front of you, allowing you to continue your forward momentum.

Tiki-taka - High probability/short passing to help a team maintain considerable possession of the ball and frustrate the other team who is given as little as 15% time of possession.

Toe Poke/Toe Blow - Striking the ball with your big toe. The toe poke is the quickest shot but often the most inaccurate.

Toe Taps - Start with the bottom of the toes of one foot on top of the ball and the other foot on the ground. Then, switch your feet so your other foot is now tapping the ball. Repeat back and forth using both feet.

Upper 90 - Either of the top corners on a net (i.e., corners are 90 degrees).

Volley - Striking the ball out of the air before it hits the ground.

V-Pull-Back - Pull the ball backward using the bottom of your foot. Then, use your other leg to push the ball and accelerate forward in the other direction (forming a "V").

Wall Passing (i.e., "1-2 Passing") - A wall pass is when you pass it to a teammate, and they pass it back to you with one touch similar to if you were to pass a ball against a wall.

Winger - Attacker who plays in the flanks. Their opposition is usually the opposing team's full backs. Their role is like an outside midfielder—except they play farther up the field and are expected to score significantly more.

Acknowledgments

I would like to thank you, the reader. I am grateful to provide you with value and help you on your journey to become a more confident soccer coach. I am happy to serve you and thank you for the opportunity to do so.

Also, I would like to recognize people who have made a difference and paved the way for me to share this book with you:

First, I want to thank my mother, who has been a role model for what can be done when you work hard towards your goals. Her work ethic and ability to overcome adversity are truly admirable, and I look up to her for this. Also, I appreciate her feedback on wording and grammatical improvements.

Second, I would like to thank the other grammar editors, Abbey Decker and Paul Marvar. Their keen eyes and terrific word choices have made the text in this book flow terrifically.

Third, I would like to thank the content editors: Kevin Solorio, Toni Sinistaj, and Youssef Hodroj. They reviewed this book for areas that could be improved and suggested additional insights to share.

Lastly, I would like to thank my soccer trainer, Aaron Byrd, whose wisdom has turned me into the soccer player and trainer that I am today. His guidance on and knowledge of this game have allowed me to pass this information on to coaches who want to grow their understanding of soccer!

Many thanks,

Made in the USA
Las Vegas, NV
10 October 2023

78886372R00066